Finding Your #UnspeakableJOY: Right There Where You Are

Finding Your
#UnspeakableJOY:
Right There Where You Are

Adrienne Fikes, M.Ed., C.S.C.
The Soul Power Coach™

The Soul Power Coach, 30 Second Challenge, Taste of Soul Power Conversation, and keyhole design are trademarks of Soul Power Coach.

Cover art by Kesha Bruce, Made of Spirit and Royal Blood 1, 2016, 48"x36", mixed media on canvas. Image courtesy of the artist and Morton Fine Art, Washington, DC.

Cover design & editing by SAH Innovations.

ISBN-13: 9781545050767
ISBN-10: 1545050767

To:

Louisa,
Susie,
Sophronia
Enezie,
Elizabeth "Lizzie",
Gladys,
Sarah Elizabeth,
Susie,
and Monica!

#GRATITUDE

Table of Contents

How You See It   8

What Is Unspeakable Joy?   21

Help Me Help You   24

Knowing Is Not Doing   26

Unspeakable Joy Is About You   28

This Is Not Just About You   30

Your Unspeakable Joy Comes First   32

You Are Stronger Than Fear   34

Set Your New Normal   37

The Sovereign Law of Roy Ayers   39

This Is Not About Me   42

Bubble Wrap and Deep Roots   44

Breathe   51

Check Yourself Log   55

Curated List of Unspeakable Joy   56

My Curated List of Unspeakable Joy   58

How God Sees It   60

#GRATITUDE   63

#GRATITUDE List   64

30 Second Soul Power Challenge™   65

Know Thy Tribe   67

So, What's Getting in the Way?   70

A Challenge Before You Go   76

Soul Power Coach™ Resources   78

Reference Notes   80

How You See It

"Our crown has already been bought and paid for. All we have to do is wear it."

–James Baldwin

You have unspeakable joy.

It's yours right now.

And I don't just mean that ordinary run of the mill 'I'm doing alright' feeling. You have genuine, down to the bone, self-generating, never-ending supply of unspeakable joy. Right there where you are. No matter who you are. No matter what you're going through. Even if you don't think you do. The truth is, all the unspeakable joy you could ever want is waiting to rise up within you, and before you're done with this book, it will begin to rise.

But don't take my word for it.

You can show yourself how this works right now.

Don't worry; you can do this sitting right where you are. Are you ready?

Wonderful!

Now as we get started, check in with yourself. Honestly, how much unspeakable joy are you feeling right now? If you were to measure how much unspeakable joy you have on a scale of 0 to 10 what number would you choose?

0 = I don't feel any unspeakable joy
10 = I am overflowing with unspeakable joy

This is important. Take a moment to select your number. Don't worry. Where ever you are is just the point where your new chapter begins. Trust the number you thought about. Write it down.

These days, I generally feel unspeakable joy at a

_____ .

In this moment, I am feeling unspeakable joy at a

_____.

Today's date is _____.

Great. Thanks for capturing this moment. It will mean more to you further down the road.

Now, let's get into this...

Take about 30 seconds to look around for the color BLUE. Anywhere blue appears - up, down, beside, behind, all around you. In any shade. Yes, out the window. There it is. Wow. You're good at this! Keep going. Where else do you see blue?

Okay, no peeking on this next part.

Close your eyes and list all the ORANGE you saw. Ah, ah! I said no peeking. Go on.
Eyes closed.

I'll wait...

Now, look around noticing the orange that you missed. Take your time.

Funny how orange was right there all along, existing simultaneously beside all of that blue. It's as if someone flipped a switch magnifying everything orange. Even tiny specks of it.

If you're on #TeamThinkingTooMuch like me, you may find yourself mentally debating if an orange-ish color counts. It counts if you want it too. Listen; there will be plenty of time for us to do *"the most"* later on. Let's stay focused here.

How is this is happening?

Why are you suddenly seeing orange in obvious and not so obvious places?

What if this is not some positive thinking gimmick, or wishful thinking or a just a fun game?

What if this is how your brain is wired?

What if you continued playing this game? What if you advanced to the next level and decided to look for all your sources of unspeakable joy instead of just seeing the color orange? What if you allowed yourself to look at you and the world in this different way?

Imagine it. How would finding your unspeakable joy make a difference in your life?

_____

_____

_____

_____

_____

What would it feel like to have a personal supply of unspeakable joy? How would you feel having as much of it as you want, whenever you want it, and more than enough to share?

I would feel _____

_____

Okay, so what if finding your unspeakable joy was a bit easier than you thought it could be? What if you always find exactly what you're looking for?

What you seek, you find.

Isn't that what is happening here? You haven't moved. Nobody snuck in while your eyes were closed to plant more orange around the room. But there it is. And there. And over there.

This is the simple, yet powerful way that your mind works.

You're noticing the color orange because your mind pays attention to whatever you tell it to see. The more you think about orange, the more you notice orange. What you give your attention to increases. What you seek, you find.

You can tell exactly what you are giving your energy to based on what you are noticing. You just showed yourself how this works by focusing your energy on seeing the color orange.

Ooh, look! Orange is still showing itself to you and you haven't done anything more than simply look for it. Even if you are in a space completely devoid of orange, you are more aware of the absence of orange than you were a moment ago.

It's just like when you were a child. Did you ever play punch buggy or the alphabet game while riding in the car? I was the youngest of five highly-energetic kids. The punch buggy game never ended, so I had to keep my eyes open looking for reasons to punch and avoid getting punched. No one likes to get caught slipping.

But punch buggy is just a game, right? Having unspeakable joy in life can't be that simple, can it?

Well yes. Yes, the decision to find unspeakable joy is that simple. Thoughts have power.

If I asked you to look for elephants or the capital letter A, or Fred Shuttlesworth, you would find yourself noticing the presence or absence of them in your vicinity. You might decide a cloud floating above looks kinda like an elephant.

Your eye would jump to notice the capital A's on and off this page. Your mind will naturally pay more attention to images and references to the late Reverend Fred Shuttlesworth, even if you do not know who he was. That attention is not a coincidence. Without giving any more thought to it, even if you don't Google him, the name Fred Shuttlesworth will begin showing up in your life.

Before you dismiss this data or decide what you think this means, all I am saying is simply that this is a reliable cognitive response. When your mind is directed to think about something, it complies. Ad agencies have used this information to sell stuff to you for ages because it works.

What you seek, you find.

That said, learning to feel unspeakable joy more

consistently is a process. Deliberately instructing your mind to find unspeakable joy means introducing new thoughts, behaviors and habits.

Listen, if your mind is going to focus on something - and it will- why not choose unspeakable joy? Why not develop the habit of seeking unspeakable joy in an ordinary day?

What you seek, you find. When you ask, your mind delivers.

"Yeah, but..."

Wait. I know where you're going. We will get there. Stay with me.

Let's think about it this way. Couldn't you choose to see and feel more of your unspeakable joy without denying, avoiding, or pretending that those other not so joyful things exist?

What I know more than anything in life is that you get exactly what you expect. Even as we acknowledge your current circumstances, isn't it possible that you have more unspeakable joy than you have allowed yourself to see or feel?

It's okay if you don't see it yet. All I'm asking you to do right now is to stay open to the possibility that this is true.

Is it possible that your mind is simply looking for other things and that you can learn exactly how to deliberately allow more unspeakable joy into your life?

_____ Yes, this is possible.

_____ No, this is impossible.

If you answered yes, you are absolutely in the right place.

The choice is yours.

It always has been.

You may not have known any of this before this moment. You may have known but didn't know exactly how to do it. No one told you. No one showed you how. You may have failed year after year trying to figure this out on your own.

You're not alone. And I want you to hear me when I say *"Nothing's wrong with you!"*

What we all have in common is that we are taught and encouraged to pay attention to our fears, uncertainty and doubts. It is part of our culture. There are so many reasons you have been convinced to focus on all that is scary and broken and bad, but not how to access and experience the genuine, never ending unspeakable joy that's been planted right there inside you.

In fact, many people I speak to about purposeful living are doing almost nothing to intentionally allow unspeakable joy to flow freely into their own lives. We feel a stronger obligation to create unspeakable joy for others, or we get caught up in policing what type or amount of joy is appropriate. We've been conditioned to think it's selfish to allow our own unspeakable joy to flow freely and consistently.

What if you are being selfish when you are NOT allowing your unspeakable joy to flow freely?

"But what good does it do to have unspeakable joy when evil, and violence, and systemic oppression are still very real?"

Great question. The thing is, if you are not firmly rooted and grounded in your own unspeakable joy, you cannot help anyone else. You have nothing authentic to share.

Think about what happens when you try. You get worn out, burned out, frustrated, disappointed, mistreated, heartbroken, sidetracked, or betrayed by the ungrateful, mean-spirited, self-centered, manipulative, ones that you are trying so desperately and unsuccessfully to help. Those exact same ones, who always need more than you have to give and continue to take your loving generosity for granted, will get angry and blame you for not doing enough.

Here's the hard truth about your relationship with them. They will never be capable of giving you your unspeakable joy. That, my powerful friend, is an inside job.

What Is Unspeakable Joy?

"The world didn't give it
The world can't take it away"

– This Joy, lyrics by Shirley Caesar

So, what am I talking about when I say unspeakable joy?

When was the last time you were bursting with joy? Does joy make you sing? Smile? Cry? Laugh? What does unspeakable joy look like when it shows up in your life?

_____

_____

_____

unspeakable joy is a magnificent, delicious state of blissful exuberance. It is a feeling that expresses your strongest state of connection with the divine, creative, loving energy of God, the Creator of the universe. In 1 Peter 1:8, the Bible defines unspeakable joy as a joy that is inexpressible and filled with glory.

You feel this joy when you are loving life because you are allowing it in. unspeakable joy is not dependent on a circumstance or a mood. This is joy that overflows, enhancing all that is beautiful and wonderful in life. It feels amazing! Who doesn't need more of that, right?

Since unspeakable joy is an inside job, you must learn how to access the unspeakable joy within you, or you might not have what's left of your peace of mind for very long.

Why is it personally important for you to find your unspeakable joy?

_____

_____

_____

The great news is, you can do this! There are amazing ways for you to find your unspeakable joy, and that's why you've got this lovely book in your hand. Here are a few things to remember as you move through this book:

Help Me Help You

Don't get me wrong, you could totally do this all on your own. It took me over forty long hard years to learn some of these strategies.

If I can do it, surely you can too. You are enough. You have enough. That said, to quote Sophia *"Don't do it Miss Celie. Don't trade places with what I've been through"* (The Color Purple, 1985).

Don't take forty more years to get this. Let me share some powerful shortcuts with you.

Now that you know better, let me help you do better – faster than you would stumbling out there alone in the dark.

Along the way you may find yourself stuck or wanting to go further. There is only so much I can share in a book and keep it short enough for you to read quickly.

If you reach a point where you could use more guidance or support to apply these strategies, I invite you to connect with me at **ww.SoulPowerCoach.Com**

Knowing Is Not Doing

There's a good chance that you have heard some of this before. I know a few sparks of insight will ignite hearing it again. It always happens. The truth is, you're not doing this actively or consistently enough.

Your inconsistency is causing you to miss out on all the unspeakable joy that you need to stay rooted and grounded on your journey. Knowing this is not the same as doing it.

Don't just to read about joy. This is a workbook of practical strategies to experience more joy at any moment you wish to feel #UnspeakableJOY.

Trust the process. It works when you actively participate. Answer the questions as we go along. You are the secret sauce for this experience.

If you come to me and say *"It didn't work"* or *"I've heard all of that before"* my first question will be – did you actively participate?

I'm a life coach. I've heard and taught it all before, yet these are a few of my personal go-to strategies that work time after time

.

Unspeakable Joy
Is About You

My hope is that these words will provide structure, valuable guidance and support for people who spend their life and energy encouraging, guiding and supporting others. I wrote this for big-hearted, grand idea-having men and women who are compelled to take chances so the world can experience the creativity that flows through them in a divine and brilliant way.

I wrote this for you because how you show up; what you create; and how you share with others are unique, beautiful, priceless gifts. These gifts demand so much energy from you because inside of you is the place where the human and the divine meet. This place is your *"Soul Power"* and unspeakable joy flows through it. You are not standing at this intersection, you are the intersection, the conduit.

You have a divine duty to be that intersection and you are worthy of the personal boundaries necessary to maintain and protect you.

Yes, what you've been called to bring forth will bless your soul in a beautiful and divine way. But you must find tried and true methods for maintaining the space for your most powerful purposeful self.

This higher self is the only version of you that is capable of being a conduit without making a serious mess of things. I'm just sayin. You want the truth or nah?

This Is Not Just About You

We both know this joy is for you but bigger than you. Why you? Because you have a true desire to lift as you climb. You know we are all connected. You understand clearly that we are one.

Your unspeakable joy is not just your divine duty, it might be a matter of life and death for someone you may never meet. Someone who is desperately waiting for your contribution.

We need creative, passionate, courageous voices like yours to stand strong, and stay in place because your gift brings the healing we need. As you are encouraged by what you learn here, you are bringing forth a precious gift that someone– maybe someone like me – needs to continue my own contribution to this community.

We need you standing in the gap, holding things down and speaking your truth in the way nobody but you can. You do not need to look far to find reasons why, now more than ever, the world need you at your post and feeling your best.

Your gifts open doors and light paths for us all. They may not be publicly celebrated, but your gifts matters. You matter. Your role in this collective is too important to the very life, health and strength of us all.

Your Unspeakable Joy Comes First

The people who love you need you, rooted, grounded and wrapped in unspeakable joy. But you won't stay in place for the duration, serving the world in the fullness of your joy, if you are not anchored in your own life. You need you first.

Look, we've both lived long enough to have learned the hard way about the personal torment that comes from not being the conduit God wants us to be. Often our response, once we stop running away, is to sacrifice our health and wellbeing, struggling in service to others. It might get the job done, but not in the best way.

unspeakable joy is what allows you to show up in service to others. If you are expecting service to bring your joy, you will quickly fall into the type of fake, manipulative benevolence that breeds resentment.

You are the most authentic, empowering conduit when you feel unspeakable joy lifting you to serve.

When you feel unspeakable joy, you show up in a magical, miraculous way. People are healed and lifted by the spirit radiating from your presence. That is the God in you challenging the God in others to rise up along with you.

You are not honoring the humanity, dignity and divine gifts in others when you are not approaching service fueled by joy.

You Are Stronger Than Fear

Storm clouds will rage. Picture a tree standing a hurricane. The stronger the roots, the more likely it is to weather the storm. Life can be a traumatic, unhappy, stressful, overwhelming, lonely, and incredibly painful place. Sometimes life can feel like an empty void. Life has, life is, and life will take you through some things. Hatred, anger, grief and despair are swallowing good, well-intentioned people whole.

James Baldwin in his 1962 New Yorker essay, Letter from a Region in My Mind, describes the pervasive stress of life as a Black American:

"One did not have to be abnormally sensitive to be worn down to a cutting edge by the incessant and gratuitous humiliation and danger one encountered every working day, all day long."

What are the forces in your life that feel like they are wearing you down? These forces can be personal or systemic.

_____

_____

_____

_____

_____

_____

_____

_____

Life is complex. Orange and blue exist simultaneously. It's perfectly okay for you to have unspeakable joy even with everything that's happening right now. You don't need permission to have unspeakable joy. There's no inappropriate time to feel unspeakable joy. And don't you dare let anyone police your emotions. I'll say more about this in a moment.

Your role is to accept the joy that is yours and allow it. I'm not asking you to create more joy right now. You may feel too much anger or grief to tackle that. I am simply inviting your joy to rise up within you. It's already there. Allow it to be what it is.

"But what about the not so joyful?"

Yes, I know. It matters. Put a pin right here. We will circle back to it. I promise.

Set Your New Normal

Finding your unspeakable joy right where you are is the first step to finding hope, peace, courage, visions for a bright future, and paths to get there. What if you could make unspeakable joy – the type of joy that rises up from within you so full, so complete, and so amazing that it is beyond anything you can describe – a consistent and self-generating staple in your everyday life? Let's create a new normal state of well being for you.

Things in your life are changing beginning here. unspeakable joy is your self-care and your self-defense. This is your line in the sand and your buffer. This is you demonstrating to you how your unspeakable joy is exponentially stronger than any circumstance you might face on your journey.

Every time you allow unspeakable joy to flow with ease, your soul has the courage and power to stand tall and speak your truth.

By the end of this book, you will know how to get rooted and grounded in your unspeakable joy. I want you to recognize where you are, no matter how far ahead, behind, or stuck in place.

This is your journey. Do not compare your journey to others. Where you are is what it is. If you feel more joy than you did before picking up this book, consider that the only win that matters.

The Sovereign Law of Roy Ayers

When my daughter was a little girl, something inappropriate or irreverent happened. I don't recall exactly what it was, but likely, it was at my expense. As she laughed, I said, *"That's not funny."* My little ray of sunshine looked up at me, and in the most sweet and sincere toddler voice, matter-of-factly said *"It's funny to meeee."*

We consider some emotions good, positive, appropriate, constructive. Other emotions we label bad, negative, inappropriate or destructive. Whatever you are feeling, let it be what it is. Do not suppress your emotions. What you feel is simply data, important data.

Your most powerful purposeful self is showing you something. The stronger the emotion the more important the message. No one – not your mama, not your partner, or your boss – no one has the right to control your emotions or tell you how you should feel. This includes anyone pushing you to be forgiving, or loving, or happy, or calm. Trying to control or dictate someone else's feelings is violent and abusive.

Do not allow anyone, not your child, or your best friend, to center themselves in your emotions. Stop suppressing whatever data your true self is giving you, so that someone else can feel more comfortable in your presence.

You can't move to where you want to be, if you refuse to acknowledge where you are. Perhaps what's really giving you the blues is your belief that it isn't okay for you to be angry about something that makes you angry. Do your very best to embrace the full range of your emotions
– without apology.

Let me be crystal clear, this is NOT a free pass to behave badly. Acting out is not okay. Kindness and anger management are good things. Being awful to others makes you awful. So don't get distracted here.

My point is, you can't analyze data or purposefully choose how to respond, if you are unable to recognize or receive the data that is coming from within you. To find your unspeakable joy, obey the Sovereign Law of Roy Ayers:

> *"Feel what you feel,*
> *When you feel what you feel,*
> *When you're feelin."*

(In the sunshine)

This Is Not About Me

My friend, you are welcome here. Although I speak freely from my personal perspective, I work with clients from all over the cultural and spiritual continuum. Your cultural experiences and a spirit-led life might look different than mine. I will not ask you to apologize for who you are, as I will not shy away from being me.

You are here to figure out how to find your unspeakable joy. If I use a word or a term that doesn't work for you, use one that does. My role here is to invite you to shift some thoughts and behaviors. As a life coach, my work leads you to your divine answers not my own. My approach with this book is no different.

If you agree to stay focused, say yes by taking a long slow breath in and out. Once more, in and out.

Sweet.

Now, let's get into it. Let's create your new amazing normal. Let's begin figuring out how you can live your ordinary days, from this day forward, feeling the fullness in every delicious bite of the unspeakable joy rising up within you.

Bubble Wrap and Deep Roots

Imagine your life buffered by a peaceful, protective cushion of bubble wrap. Circumstances still hit, but they don't hit as hard. Things that would've knocked you down, barely register in your mind. Even when you get knocked down, getting back up seems easier than it was. How awesome that there is a calm place of clarity, comfort and assurance in the midst of a raging storm.

I've always admired the courage and composure of civil rights advocates like Ida B. Wells, Fannie Lou Hamer, C.T. Vivian and Fred Shuttlesworth. All fierce in their resolve to advocate for black dignity and humanity. Somehow, they managed not to get consumed by the anger and fear that is a perfectly reasonable human response to the unchecked, unpredictable domestic terrorism of lynch mobs, beatings, and bombs. Think about it. You know how angry we can get just sitting in a traffic jam. So how did they do it?

These African American women and men are strategic, passionate voices of liberation and power, standing tall against white supremacist hatred.

Rev. Fred Shuttlesworth's biography, *"A Fire You Can't Put Out"* (Manis, 1999), talks about the terrorist attack on his church parsonage Christmas Day in 1956. That afternoon, Rev. Shuttlesworth and his family had returned home from visiting one of his daughters, who was hospitalized after a serious home accident.

As his wife and other children relaxed in the living room, a bomb was thrown at the house. Somewhere between six and sixteen sticks of dynamite exploded at the bedroom window where Fred Shuttlesworth was stretched across the bed. Miraculously, he survived with just a bump on his head, unharmed by the fireball and wood splinters that shot up from the floor.

His biography says *"Spiritually, something irreversible had happened to him."*

Shuttlesworth emerged from the wreckage of his bombed home, more resolved than ever to lead what would become the Birmingham Civil Rights Campaign, saying:

"If God could keep me through all of this, then I'm here for the duration."

We need you here for the duration too. What I understand about the movement Rev. Shuttlesworth led is that each campaign began with bubble wrap and deep roots. Every activist, began their direct actions by opening that connection to the Source of power and love.

Before confronting government-sponsored terrorists, vicious dogs, fire hoses, bombs, chains, bats, and brass knuckles, these world changers rooted and grounded themselves in unspeakable joy. They reminded themselves of their divine purpose and wrapped themselves in prayer and spiritual songs.

The courage and peace to step out on faith is called up from within you.

But what would that look like in your situation? The challenges you have might not seem as frightening, or maybe they do. How do you call forth your own metaphysical strength to face challenges in your life? How can you stay rooted and grounded when things that wear you down take a turn for the worse? My powerful friend, you have already started this process.

> *"You've been my joy in the time of sorrow*
> *Hope for my tomorrow*
> *Peace in a time of storm*
> *Strength when I'm weak and worn"*

> *– You've Been So Faithful,*
> *lyrics by Eddie James*

In this moment, I'm feeling unspeakable joy at a
_____ (0-10).

Today is _____ .

You may notice that you are already beginning to feel a bit more joy. Don't be put off by the simplicity of what is happening here. Just because it is simple doesn't make it less powerful. In the same way that water refreshes you, a cool breeze feels good, and the sun on your face makes you feel warm, some things just are.

Now here's where you begin taking the lead as you move along in your search for unspeakable joy. You get to choose which way to go. Always begin with the most important strategy - Breathe. From there, you can choose to read the strategies in order, or you might need to jump around as you see fit. Beginning your adventure with Breathe will help you assess how much joy you are feeling. From there, you will know where you need to go next.

Don't forget to trust the process as we go along. That means if you skipped over rating your joy a few pages ago, back up to do that now.

Every step I'm asking you to take matters. I am using a *"Don't talk about it, be about it"* method to share proven strategies based on the research and applications of behavior modification and human development. These strategies will help you get rooted and grounded in joy. Some are meant to help you feel better right now, giving you a boost to let in more unspeakable joy immediately. All the strategies work like roots of a majestic tree, anchors growing strong and deep to nourish your soul with joy.

Remember:

- Developing your new normal level of unspeakable joy will take time.

- Answering the questions as you go will help you track your progress.

- Doing the strategies in this book will help you feel grounded.

- Practicing these strategies will help you stay rooted.

- Always begin with Breathe.

Breathe

As a little girl, my niece had regular asthma attacks. When she had trouble breathing, this nebulizer, a portable box of tubes, wires and a tiny little mask, treated her airways and lungs allowing her to get back to a place where she could breathe on her own.

This box was a necessary, life-saving travel companion that became a normal part of our life. If she was having trouble breathing, everything stopped until we knew her airways were unconstricted.

As she grew older, her mom began involving her in physical activities like dance and basketball. Over the years, as she stretched her lung capacity and grew stronger, her use of the nebulizer decreased thanks to that active lifestyle.

Today she is a fiercely-talented professional ballerina with incredible strength and stamina. I don't remember when my sister stopped carrying around that contraption. I do remember the day my niece lifted my sister's couch with her toes! The change was gradual.

The first and most important strategy I'd like you to practice for the rest of your life is to ask yourself,

"Am I breathing?"

The term unspeakable joy itself is a direct challenge to your present state of being. It's an audacious, commanding standard of joy, beyond what we typically accept as normal. You wonder why I keep asking you to think about and rate your state of unspeakable joy as we move through. If you are completely satisfied with your present level, fabulous. If you're less than satisfied, checking yourself serves as a call to action.

Do you have unspeakable joy? Some days this question will be cause for celebration. Other days it will be a challenge to do something. Only you can decide what it means to you in that moment. I compare unspeakable joy to breathing, because, even if you don't think about breathing, your natural impulse is to breathe. Anything that happens to hinder or arrest your breathing is a problem. When you ask *"Am I breathing?"* you might answer:

"I was breathing."
"I am breathing."
"I will be breathing."

Only one of those responses is okay. The other responses, if they persist for more than a moment, will quickly prove how detrimental they are.

Like breathing, feeling unspeakable joy allows you to inhale love, peace, art, music and laughter. Joy makes it easier to exhale courage, energy, motivation, focus, organization, resilience, and more good feeling thoughts. It's a cycle. In and out.

In this very moment, yes right now, if your unspeakable joy is not already high or rising from the rating at the beginning of this book, pick one of the strategies to help you restore or raise your level of unspeakable joy. Then use the Check Yourself Log on page 55 to rate your unspeakable joy again.

This is important. The lower your present level of unspeakable joy, the more likely your mood is resistant to receiving this information.

It's okay to be just a bit skeptical and feel some reluctance. Strong negative feelings work just like airway obstructions, blocking your joy. What you are thinking and feeling colors the decisions you make. Fear is separation from and obstruction of your soul power. God does not speak to you through fear.

Fear is a signal to reconnect and let your unspeakable joy flow. Set yourself up to make more purposeful decisions. If you need it, take time right now for an emotional nebulizer treatment.

"And you gotta know
The story is still to be told
Just breathe
Remember to breathe"

– Breathe, lyrics by Lalah Hathaway

Check Yourself Log

*"Chickity-check yo self
Before you wreck yo self"*

– Check Yo Self, lyrics by Ice Cube

How much unspeakable joy are you feeling   right now?

Day	Scale (0–10)	Day	Scale (0-10)

Curated List of Unspeakable Joy

The most helpful strategy I've ever used to find my joy is a curated list of unspeakable joy. This is a personally crafted list of things you can do at any moment to ease your spirit back into a purposeful place, allowing your unspeakable joy to flow freely.

On a daily basis, I use at least two or three items on this list to bubble wrap me in joy. Stay ready so you don't have to get ready, right? If I have strong negative emotions, like grief or worry, I know I'm not thinking clearly. I can easily pick anything off my list to level off and begin to get my unspeakable joy flowing freely again.

Even though a sunny spot at a private, beachfront island villa is my ultimate happy place, that is not on my list. Include items that do not require you to spend money, or board planes, or phone a friend to do. You need a few items that could be done within a few minutes – right from your desk, or on the move. If you're around other people, it's possible they wouldn't even realize what you are really doing.

Admiring a lovely piece of art, connecting good people to each other, wonderful scents, hearing beautiful music, and moving your body can lift your soul immediately. These simple joys serve as powerful bubble wrap – emotional nebulizers – to get you back on track.

How would you complete your own curated list of joys? Take a moment to add a few tried and true sources of joy to your curated list. What are mental or physical things you can do at any moment, to bring you joy? Again, this is about you. You do not need anyone else's approval or permission to find your unspeakable joy. Focus on listing simple items then use interesting combinations to mix things up, exponentially multiplying your joy.

My Curated List of Unspeakable Joy

"When you feel down and out
Sing a song
It'll make your day"

– Sing a Song, lyrics by Maurice White

and Al McKay of Earth, Wind & Fire

Things I can do at any moment to lift my spirit and allow my unspeakable joy to flow freely.

_____

_____

_____

_____

_____

_____

_____

_____

_____

Toward the end of 2015, I commissioned DJ Stylus, The Vibe Conductor, to create a series of four quarterly music mixes around my favorite themes – Peace, Courage, Love and Freedom.

Our friend Maceo, an art broker, paired original artwork from local DC artists with the themes of each mixtape.

This project turned into The Listening Party, a sensory collaboration for fine art collectors who love music and are on a path of personal growth. The Listening Party happy hours allowed us to feel a greater sense of peace; mix with good people; and make powerful purposeful decisions – a great mix of items from my list!

If The Listening Party mixes are something you might enjoy, download The Listening Party: Volumes 1-4 from DJ Stylus' website at:

VibeConductor.Com/tag/soul-power-coach

These mixes are awesome, free, and will likely introduce you to some wonderful creative artists.

How God Sees It

If you want to find your unspeakable joy right there where you are, you'll need to see more things as God sees them. God says *"My thoughts are not your thoughts, neither are your ways my ways."*

-Isaiah 55:8

When you feel resistance to this idea, remind yourself of times when you didn't see things God's way. You've learned and grown from God's wisdom and divine sight in the past. Remind yourself of how you saw things 3-5 years ago and where you've changed:

Back then, I was sure I knew _____

_____

_____

I was afraid to _____

_____

_____

At first, I could not _____

_____

_____

but now I've learned _____

_____

_____

I thought I wanted _____

_____

_____

but now I know _____

_____

_____

_____

_____ is

easy now but was difficult for me back then.

Look at all God has kept you through. Finding your unspeakable joy means dealing with the stubbornness and controlling nature that makes us act as if we know it all (I said we, don't sit there as if it's just me).

The audacious commanding level of unspeakable joy that you deserve comes naturally when you choose to see circumstances, people and problems as God sees them. Ask to see things differently. God will give you the vision.

#GRATITUDE

Challenging yourself to focus on gratitude is like choosing to focus on orange instead of blue. Use a scrap of paper or record them in a journal. You can even use your fingers to count off.

Name 20 reasons to feel gratitude. They can be big reasons or small. 20 reasons for you to feel gratitude in this moment.

If you are struggling name at least 20 reasons to feel gratitude, keep going until you name 30.

Yes 30. Stretch your mind. Remember, gradual changes are powerful.

#GRATITUDE LIST

"I wanna thank you for your love (Thank you)
Thank you for your power (Thank you)
Thank you for protection (Thank you)
Every hour"

– Thank You Lord,
lyrics by Walter Hawkins

1.	11.	21.
2.	12.	22.
3.	13.	23.
4.	14.	24.
5.	15.	25.
6.	16.	26.
7.	17.	27.
8.	18.	28.
9.	19.	29.
10.	20.	30.

30 Second
Soul Power Challenge™

You are already making decisions every day, every moment about your highest priorities. Finding your unspeakable joy starts with knowing what is most important to you. Having purposeful priorities helps you figure out where your boundaries, focus, time and energy need to be.

It's time to set your purposeful priorities before you make any more decisions. This fun challenge clears your head, tests your decision-making skills and shifts you back into unspeakable joy by reminding you of your highest intentions and short term goals. When you need a quick strategy, if things get overwhelming, or you feel stuck, this challenge quickly gives you clarity and a sense of direction based on what is most important to you. You remember you, don't you?

You know, that one person in your life you forget to think about.

Start setting better personal boundaries now. Take my 30 Second Soul Power Challenge™ free at **SoulPowerCoach.Com/30Seconds**

Know Thy Tribe

Personal growth is not just about working on yourself. Yes, allowing yourself to find unspeakable joy means accepting yourself as a whole and complete person.

It also means reflecting on the whole and complete people who are in your tribe, for better or worse, no matter how amazing, distant, or volatile the relationships may be. You are related – energetically and inextricably connected – to your immediate and extended family. They are your tribe of origin and what you understand about them shapes how you see yourself. How could you understand your unique life detached from its historical context? Keeping our previous rules of engagement in mind, here are two simple, yet powerful ways to know thy tribe:

Family Photo Ops

Pull out the family albums, dust off the boxes in storage. Gather a few relatives and go through old pictures together. They probably have pictures you have not seen. Mix it up between immediate and distant relatives. Ask questions. Share stories. Linger. Listen. Heal. Repeat.

No Family, No Photos, No Problem

Even if you are the last member of your tribe, and there are no family photos around, systemic influences shape our lives. Many of our triumphs and challenges are shared experiences. These socioeconomic, cultural and regional norms shape your options and choices and those of your tribe. If you are not making intentional life choices, someone is making them for you.

Here are four amazing resources to begin learning how these systemic forces shaped your life and your family history:

- Isabel Wilkerson's Pulitzer Prize winning book *The Warmth of Other Suns* (2011)
- Michelle Alexander's book *The New Jim Crow* (2010)
- Ava Duvernay's Oscar-nominated documentary 13th (2016)
- Smithsonian's National Museum of African American History and Culture

.

So, What's Getting in the Way?

Earlier, I invited you to put a pin in discussing all of the not so joyful things that may be happening in your life. If you can remember to just check yourself and breathe, you've already started winning. But finding unspeakable joy is not just about handling stress, it is about thriving like a majestic oak in both sunshine and rain. This is about loving life even when life feels like it does not love you. I am not inviting you to sacrifice yourself to a struggle. You can transcend and transform the struggle through your unspeakable joy.

Just because orange and blue exist simultaneously, doesn't mean you are powerless to do anything about that blue. Just because your life may seem to have more blue than orange, doesn't mean you need to continue living that way. Breathe. Ask. Receive.

Don't be afraid to face those fears. unspeakable joy transforms darkness.

In April 2016, Rev. Dr. Barbara A. Holmes delivered a powerful sermon during a Howard University School of Divinity conference on religion and science saying:

"There are different kinds of darkness... I'm referring to the darkness that pervades the womb out of which all of us are born. This is a mothering darkness that nurtures its offspring, and is a Source of life... The darkness that I speak of is rich and God- filled, healing and preventative, powerful and cohesive."

-(Howard University. April 2016)

You cannot find the fullness of joy if you are afraid of the dark. Now, I can't tell you those less than joyful things will ever change or even go away. What I do know for sure is that you will change.

That change in you will help root you and ground you to your unspeakable joy.

Imagine your normal state of unspeakable joy sits at a 4 on a scale of 0-10. What happens when something hits, knocking you back 3 points? How are you equipped to respond to that same circumstance if your new normal becomes a 7 or a 10?

Getting comfortable with your new normal likely means exploring the seven points of purposeful decisions in a meaningful way

Somewhere along this continuous cycle, you are getting in your own way. Most people are aware of the results they have and want in their life. Your results are determined by the beliefs you hold, like the rules you have about what is possible and what

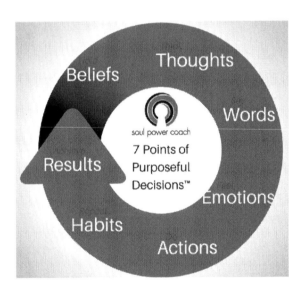

you deserve. Your thoughts, words, and feelings are the ingredients that create your actions. Habits are actions you regularly repeat. All these points influence the results you see in your life. To create new results, pay attention to the data. You are showing yourself exactly what needs to be addressed in your life. Your inner wisdom, your divine soul power is the best guidance ever.

If you need more support with this, that is a more extensive conversation than we are having here. Check the resources at the back of this book and visit **SoulPowerCoach.Com/Talk** to request a Taste of Soul Power Conversation.

Each and every purposeful decision you make from here allows your joy to flow freely, lifting you higher and higher until your joy – even on an ordinary day – is #UnspeakableJOY.

"Jazz is makin' do with 'taters and grits
Standin' up each time you get hit
Jazz ain't nothing' but soul"

– Jazz, by Betty Carter

In this moment, I'm feeling unspeakable joy at a

_____(0-10).

What do I want to remember about this information?
How was this useful for me?

_____

_____

_____

_____

_____

_____

_____

_____

_____

_____

What will I do differently now that I know how to find my unspeakable joy?

_____

_____

_____

What support do I need to hold myself accountable for all the things I want to do differently?

_____

_____

_____

_____

_____

_____

_____

_____

_____

_____

A Challenge
Before You Go

"And the energy will absorb
Power for the metaphysical one"

– Cloud 9, lyrics by Donnie

I wouldn't be the Soul Power Coach™ if I didn't issue a challenge to you before you go. Your challenge is to Check Yourself, for the next 90 days.

If you are *"breathing"* unspeakable joy, celebrate!

If you're not *"breathing"* let it serve as an immediate call to action to revisit these strategies and resources.

Let me know how finding your unspeakable joy, right there where you are, seems easier than it did when you first picked up this book.

My social media profile is:

Adrienne **@SoulPowerCoach**.

Reach out. Share your success stories and insights with me using #UnspeakableJOY on Twitter, Instagram, LinkedIn, or Facebook. You may also email **info@soulpowercoach.com**

You deserve a life overflowing not just with joy, but with #UnspeakableJOY.

Here's To Your **#UnspeakableJOY**,

Adrienne, the Soul Power Coach™

Soul Power Coach™ Resources

Take the 30 Second Soul Power Challenge™ at:
SoulPowerCoach.Com/30Seconds

Request a complimentary Taste of Soul Power Conversation at:

SoulPowerCoach.Com/Talk

Download all four of The Listening Party Mixtapes by DJ Stylus – The Vibe Conductor Volume 1: Peace, Volume 2: Courage, Volume 3: Love, Volume 4: Freedom

VibeConductor.Com/tag/soul-power-coach

Reference Notes

Alexander, Michelle. (2010). *The New Jim Crow: Mass incarceration in the age of colorblindness*. New York: [Jackson, Tenn.]:New Press; Distributed by Perseus Distribution,

Averick, Spencer, Duvernay, A., Barish, H. (Producer) Duvernay, A (Director) (2016). *13TH* (Documentary) World Wide: Netflix.

Ayers, R. (1976). Everybody Loves the Sunshine. (Recorded by Roy Ayers). On Everybody Loves The Sunshine (Album). Location: Polydor.(1976)

Baldwin, James. (1962, November 17). *Letter from a region in my mind.* The New Yorker. **www.newyorker.com/magazine/1962/11/17/letter-from-a-region-in-my-mind**

Caesar, S. (2013). This Joy (Recorded by Shirley Caesar). On A Miracle In Harlem [CD]. Location: Sonorous Entertainment, Inc. (2013)

Cube, I. (1993). Check Yo Self. (Recorded by Ice Cube featuring Das EFX). On The Predator. [CD]. Location: Priority (1993)

Donnie. (2003) Cloud 9. (Recorded by Donnie). On The Colored Section [CD]. Location: Giant Steps (2003)

Hathaway, L., Rideout, R., Rippol, R. (2008). Breathe. (Recorded by Lalah Hathaway). On Self-Portrait [CD]. Location: Stax. (2008)

Hawkins, W. (1990) Thank You Lord. (Recorded by Walter Hawkins featuring Rev. Yvette Flunder and the Love Center Choir). On Love Alive IV [CD]. Location: Malaco. (1990)

Holmes, Dr. Barbara A. (Guest Minister). (2106, April 7). *When the Force Awakens: Dark Hope, Cosmic Power.* HUSD Religion & Science Chapel [Video file]. Howard University School of Divinity Religion and Science Conference Chapel Service. Retrieved from **youtu.be/7V9grT16Vlk**

James, E. (2001) You've Been So Faithful. (Recorded by Eddie James and the Phoenix Mass Choir). On Higher [CD]. Location: Malaco Records. (2001)

Manis. Andrew M. (1999). *A Fire You Can't Put Out: The Civil Rights Life Of Birmingham's Reverend Fred Shuttlesworth.* Tuscaloosa. The University of Alabama Press.

Mapp, N. (1992) Jazz Ain't Nuthin But Soul. (Recorded by Betty Carter). On I Can't Help It [CD]. Location: Impulse!/GRP (1992)

Smithsonian's National Museum of African American History and Culture. District of Columbia. **nmaahc.si.edu**

Spielberg, S. (Director). (1985). The Color Purple [Motion picture]. Amblin, Guber-Peters, WB.

White, M., McKay, A. (1975). Sing a Song. (Recorded by Earth, Wind & Fire). On Gratitude [Album]. Location: Columbia. (1975)

Wilkerson, Isabel. (2011). The Warmth Of Other Suns: The Epic Story of America's Great Migration. New York: Random House.

44338466R00049

Made in the USA
Middletown, DE
03 June 2017